For the Love of Reading

By Valerie Bendt

Other books by Valerie Bendt:
How to Create Your Own Unit Study
The Unit Study Idea Book
Success with Unit Studies
Creating Books with Children
The Frances Study Guide

Chapter Title Pages Illustrated by Michelle Bendt, Age 14

Proofread by Nancy Crowson and Bruce Bendt

Copyright 1994, by Valerie Bendt

Cover Photo © Arthur Tilley / FPG International Corp.

P.O. Box 1365
8786 Highway 21
Melrose, FL 32666

ISBN 1-885814-00-3

DEDICATION

I dedicate this book to my daughter, Melissa, and my mother, Hope Connelly, who both graciously worked on typing the manuscript of this book from my handwritten copy. I know that deciphering my scrawl was not an easy task. Thanks!

TABLE OF CONTENTS

INTRODUCTION

There are numerous reading programs available to enable you to teach your children to read. These programs vary in content. Some have: workbooks, games, activities, phonetic readers, spoken audio tapes, sing-a-long audio tapes, and teacher's manuals. There are programs to suit most every type of learner. There are programs to suit most every type of instructor. Many of these programs are geared to teach writing, composition, and spelling, too. In a society where we are inundated with so many reading programs, why am I writing still another book about reading? My desire is to share my experiences in teaching my children to read. I want to show you how you can personalize your reading program so your children not only learn the mechanics of reading, but they develop a love for reading, a love that will cause them to be life-long readers and, therefore, life-long learners.

It is my hope that the children learn to be expressive and creative at an early age, or rather I should say, that their creativity and expressiveness that are so ripe at an early age be encouraged to blossom rather than be discouraged by too formal and stilted a program.

Reading is an important part of our entire lives. Let it be an enjoyable, integral part right from the start. And for those with older children who need motivation to read, hopefully some of the ideas set forth in this book will provide an avenue by which to nurture the desire to make reading an important part of their lives as well.

CHAPTER ONE
An Idea is Born

An Idea is Born

Unfortunately, the first child in a family is often taught by the trial and error method. This has been the case with my oldest daughter, Michelle. My husband and I knew we would homeschool our children even before they were born. We didn't exactly know how, but we knew in our hearts that it was the best practice for our family. Back in the early days of homeschooling there were few voices offering instruction to parents desiring to homeschool, so we were terribly excited by any materials we could locate on the subject. Through a friend we found out about a Christian correspondence school that would accept homeschooled children. We enrolled Michelle immediately when she reached the acceptable age of four years. I was so excited that she was finally old enough to homeschool. (Years later I realized that I had been successfully homeschooling her before her official enrollment. After the enrollment, our methods began to digress.)

I very promptly induced this independent, creative, intelligent child to sit quietly and complete X number of worksheets, in a given period of time, for five days each week. She rebelled almost instantly. "Mommy this is boring. Mommy I know this stuff already." But like the thorough mother that I am, I insisted that she complete *every* page. After all, she might miss a concept or a rule which might tarnish her academically for life.

Now during this time period, I was doing my homework, being careful to learn every phonetic rule. I didn't concern myself with math too much because it was a favorite subject of mine, and I had already had several years experience in tutoring children in math. Phonics presented somewhat of a problem, not because I wasn't a good reader, but because I wasn't familiar with the rules of the game.

After applying myself diligently to the mastery of the rules, I needed a subject on which to try out this newly acquired knowledge. Naturally, Michelle was my target, but the problem was that by the age of four and a half she was burned out on schoolwork. I can't

Unfortunately, the first child in a family is often taught by the trial and error method.

Phonics presented somewhat of a problem, not because I wasn't a good reader, but because I wasn't familiar with the rules of the game.

fully describe what happened as Michelle progressed from age four to four and a half, but the following incident may give you some idea.

As I explained earlier, Michelle is a very creative child. She loves to draw and make things out of paper. One day during her fourth year, she was supposed to be completing her worksheets, and I was rather upset with her because she couldn't read. After all, she was four and a half and according to the teacher's manual, she should have been reading by now! I could see her academic future being washed down the drain. Ready to give up, I left her in the dining room with her pencils, scissors, and paper and decided to read to her little sister, Melissa, who was two and a half years old at the time. Melissa wanted to be read to all of her waking hours, and I decided that this was a comfortable idea as I was pregnant with our third child.

Melissa and I sat in the rocking chair reading in the living room while Michelle busied herself in the adjacent dining room. Michelle had given up the phonics workbooks in favor of creating doll house furnishings from paper. Let me further describe what she was doing. Michelle would draw a figure on her paper, cut it out, fold it, tape the ends, and produce a china hutch, television, chairs, washer and dryer, and so forth.

Meanwhile, Melissa and I were reading. By this time Melissa had learned the alphabet and now she was working on learning the sounds those letters generally make when used at the beginning of a word (initial consonant sounds). She then progressed to detecting the letter sounds at the end of a word (final consonant sounds). As I read to Melissa, I casually pointed out the letters in some of the words and emphasized their sounds. Next we worked on short vowel sounds in words like *cat, dog, cup, pig,* and *bed*. Melissa loved this attention and progressed rapidly. (After all, this was really just a game to her.) Michelle was taking all this in from the other room, more extensively than I realized.

I began pointing out more difficult phonetic combinations to

Melissa like *bl, cl, fr, tr,* and other blends. Later she was ready for the more complex phonetic sounds like *oo, ow, ou,* and *or* that appear in the middle of words. I would say to Melissa, for example, "See this word, *f-o-o-d,* well, *oo* says *oo* in this word. The word is *food.* Then I would point out other *oo* words, still rather casually, as we read along. Days, and probably weeks passed, and each day I would sit and read with Melissa and Michelle would draw or create something out of paper.

It wasn't long before Michelle was interrupting as I read with Melissa in the next room, and she was shouting out the sounds for the letter combinations that we were reviewing. Melissa was learning to read in a pleasurable relaxed way on Mother's lap, and Michelle was learning to read by eavesdropping! (I'm convinced that if your child is having difficulty with a concept, go in the next room, whisper the information, and he will get it.)

This teaching strategy benefited Melissa, Michelle, and me. Melissa wanted to be coddled and read to, Michelle wanted to be free to work with her hands, and I needed to be able to share this new phonetic knowledge that I had acquired with someone!

Things haven't changed much through the years in our household. While I'm reading aloud to my children, Melissa still wants to look over my shoulder and read along, and Michelle listens better if her hands are busy either drawing or sewing, and I still have a need to share new thoughts and ideas with them. I learned an important lesson 10 years ago from our first schooling experiences; I learned that children are individuals. They have varying needs, desires, strengths, and weaknesses. I learned to be flexible while still remaining goal oriented. My goals have not varied too much over the years; however, my teaching strategies have varied to fit the needs of my children and our family's situation.

I learned that I couldn't recreate school in the home effectively and more importantly that I shouldn't! If anything, the schools should be trying to emulate the atmosphere prevalent in the home. I used to look back on the early years of homeschooling and feel a sense of

Melissa was learning to read in a pleasurable relaxed way on Mother's lap, and Michelle was learning to read by eavesdropping!

I learned to be flexible while still remaining goal oriented.

I learned that I couldn't recreate school in the home effectively and more importantly that I shouldn't!

failure. But I've come to look on those years as a growing period, a period of growth and learning for me, my husband, and my children. What's important is that we grow as a family and learn from our experiences.

I would like to relate another situation that occurred while teaching my son Robert to read. When Robert was five years old, I began teaching him to combine letter sounds to form short words like *cat, dog, bit, rug,* and *bell.* After he had fairly mastered some simple words like these, I handed him a small, very easy, phonetically controlled reader. One of the pages in the book read something like, "Hop Fred, hop, hop, hop." He dutifully proceeded to read the book when suddenly he looked at me quite frustrated and said, "Mom, people don't really talk like that!"

I was astounded at this five-year-old's perceptiveness, and I decided that I wouldn't offend his intelligence by having him plod through such monotonous books any longer. I said, "Robert, would you like to write your own readers?" He quickly agreed to this and I immediately asked him to dictate a story to me. Still not sure what was to be the outcome of this, but delighted that he wasn't going to have to read anymore little readers, Robert began enthusiastically telling me a story.

I carefully wrote each word, inserting proper capitalization and punctuation as I went along meticulously forming each letter. I had large Kindergarten-lined paper on hand, so this is what I chose to transcribe his story. After he dictated about 6 or 8 pages to me, I read his story to him and had him draw a picture to accompany his story. Then I handed the papers to him and said, "Now, here is your reader. Read it to me."

Robert exclaimed, "Why, I can't read that, it's too hard!" I reminded him that he wrote the story, so how could it be too hard for him to read? (Put in that manner, it did sound logical to him.) He skeptically took the pages from me and slowly began to read the words. Suddenly, the story began to flow more naturally and a bright smile came over his face. When he reached a difficult word he managed to decipher it. After all, it was his story, so he was familiar with the story line and the vocabulary. Occasionally, I would help him with a word or two. Robert and I were both so excited that we could hardly contain ourselves. He had progressed in one sitting from reading sentences like, "Hop Fred, hop, hop, hop," to reading sentences like, "The knight lived in the dazzling castle on the hill."

Our excitement was contagious, and Raymond, who was only three years old at the time, was anxious to "tell Mommy a story, too." Well, I carefully wrote out Raymond's story, and then I read it to him. Afterward, I let him illustrate his story. I began to see how successful this teaching method could be. In only six months, Robert progressed from reading on a Kindergarten level to reading on a third-grade level. (I confess, I succumbed to temptation and pulled out a third-grade reader which Robert read flawlessly. He also noted that these stories were much more interesting than those in the beginning readers.)

Not only did this simple method of reading instruction produce a terrific reader, it produced two terrific storytellers. Yes, every time Robert dictated a story, little Raymond had to dictate a *longer* story. And out of this love for storytelling arose a desire to make books, real books.

I want to explain that I did continue giving Robert phonics instruction using a manual that supplied me with appropriate exercises. We would spend a short time each week on mastering the rules and the remainder of the time Robert would spend dictating stories and reading them to me.

We also played games to help with difficult sounds. Most of these were card games that I made up, but more recently I've found a book called, **Games for Reading**, by Peggy Kaye. This book includes over 75 easy-to-make games that are not only fun to play, but that are beneficial for building the child's vocabulary, for helping him to hear letter sounds more accurately, and for training his eye to see patterns of letters. I find that I am more consistent in using games that I make rather than using purchased games, because I already have time invested in the game. My children seem to appreciate that I've taken the time to make something for them, and many times they are also able to help make the games, which makes them even more valuable!

As Peggy Kaye states:

Games put children in exactly the right frame of mind for learning difficult things. Children throw themselves into playing games the way they never throw themselves into filling out workbook pages.[1]

Combine your favorite reading program with *Games for Reading*, have your child write (dictate) his own readers, and you will have a winning phonics program, a program that encourages creativity and a love for reading!

CHAPTER TWO
To Invent Stories, You Need to Listen to Stories

To Invent Stories, You Need to Listen to Stories

Robert and Raymond's ability to create stories didn't just happen in a day or two. For a number of years my husband, my two older daughters, and I had been reading to them daily. They also listened to stories on audio cassette tapes. Story time was part of our daily routine (and it continues to be). This story time included selections from picture books, novels, biographies, poetry books, Bible stories, the Bible, and numerous other kinds of books. They had assimilated many stories, and when asked to compose stories of their own, they had little trouble. Occasionally, they would be stumped when they could not evoke the right name for a character or place. But, after a little contemplation, they would devise a satisfactory title.

Recently, my son Robert who is now ten years old, was dictating a poem to me for inclusion in one of his most recent books entitled, **Fine Art Pictures and Poems**. First, I allowed him to brainstorm, thinking of many words that related to his poem's topic. After compiling a list which he dictated to me, I encouraged him to think of words that rhyme with the words in his list, and I wrote these down also. It was then time for him to compose the poem. We sat for what seemed a very long time with no utterance from Robert. I guess I displayed a sense of annoyance as I told him I would be back after I did some laundry. When I came back, he dictated a simple but excellent poem to accompany his re-creation of Monet's painting entitled, **Houses of Parliament**. Robert's poem reads as follows:

> **The River Thames**
> On the quiet River Thames,
> The House of Parliament sits,
> The fog and bog surrounding it,
> Enclosed in gloom and mist.

They had assimilated many stories, and when asked to compose stories of their own, they had little trouble.

11

So now when I try to hurry my children or press them too hard, I remember, "There are some things that are worth waiting for!"

I was obviously impressed with his poem and Robert smiled and said, "Now Mom, some things are worth waiting for!" So now when I try to hurry my children or press them too hard, I remember, "There are some things that are worth waiting for!"

A mother who attended one of my seminars related an interesting story to me. She said her family was studying the fruits of the Spirit and her little daughter said, "Mommy, I can tell you all the fruits of the Spirit." She began, "Love, joy, peace, patience, kindness, goodness, hope, gentleness, self-control, and *hurrying*." Her mother was rather astounded and said, "Hurrying?" Her daughter explained, "Oh, yes, I figure that's the most important one because you're always telling us to hurry, hurry!" That mother said that now when she catches herself hurrying her children, she stops and remembers that her time with them is really very short, and that she must make the time to enjoy them.

It's important for us to consider these thoughts when teaching our children, whether it's teaching them how to read, or how to tie their shoes. We should not be speeding our children on to adulthood, but rather nurturing, loving, and just enjoying them.

We should not be speeding our children on to adulthood, but rather nurturing, loving, and just enjoying them.

"Children are a gift from the Lord, the fruit of the womb is His reward."

CHAPTER THREE
Providing an Atmosphere for Learning

Providing an Atmosphere for Learning

Naturally, very young children seldom have the necessary attention span to sit through an entire book. Even a simple board book may be overwhelming for an adventuresome youngster. Some (like my daughter Melissa) will show an interest in books at an early age, but many are too busy with important matters like building block towers, or more often, un-building (otherwise known as knocking down) block towers built by someone else.

I learned through the years of homeschooling my children how stimulating it is for young children to be present when their older siblings are having their lessons. Often the very young are busy at play while I'm reading aloud to the older children. It's amazing to me how much they absorb even though they aren't planted next to me on the sofa while I'm reading. We often think that the children must be sitting close by with eyes fastened to us or the book. (Remember the incident I related earlier about Michelle learning to read by over-hearing?)

Last spring, as I was preparing for a workshop, I was selecting library books to use during my presentation. My daughter, Mandy, who was three and a half years old at the time, had accompanied me to the library. As I pulled a copy of **The Story of My Life**, by Helen Keller from the shelf, Mandy looked at the photograph on the cover and exclaimed, "That's Helen Keller. You read that book to us." I was astonished at this remark, for Mandy was only two years old when I read the book to my children.

Mandy has absorbed much information by being in the room during schooling hours. Her experiences are not confined to traditional preschool lessons, but to real literature, history, science, math, and so on. Preschool subjects are taught naturally through daily life experiences. Mandy didn't complete a series of worksheets on squares to learn about squares. Squares and other preschool topics were a part of her real world.

I learned through the years of homeschooling my children how stimulating it is for young children to be present when their older siblings are having their lessons.

Her experiences are not confined to traditional preschool lessons, but to real literature, history, science, math, and so on.

People sometimes ask, "What type of kindergarten program do you have planned for Mandy?" Well, she already enjoys sign language, spouting off definitions for Greek and Latin roots, learning about electricity and magnetism, dictating and illustrating stories (her art work is somewhat non-descript as she spent too much time studying Picasso), *typing* on the computer, learning about Ancient Egypt, and more. I guess she will keep on learning right along with the rest of the family!

Mandy didn't have much of an interest in the alphabet in printed form before age four, but she was very intrigued by the manual sign alphabet. Now as I sign the alphabet, she can say the names for each letter that I sign, regardless of the order in which I sign them. I initially taught her the *A, B, C Song*, signing each letter as I sang the names for the letters. Recently she has begun making the signs for the letters with her own chubby hands. It may seem unusual, but she has learned the manual sign alphabet before learning the printed form. The printed form will be mastered later. Incidentally, I am using her knowledge of the manual sign alphabet to teach her the printed letters and their sounds. (I don't recommend this procedure for all children, but I mention it to emphasize that it is beneficial to use a child's interests to teach him basic skills.)

All my children have learned their alphabet with help from *Dr. Seuss's ABC* book. (We are presently on our second copy.) Now as I read this book with Mandy, I make the letter sign with my right hand and point with my left hand to the corresponding letter on the page. Then Mandy proudly tells me the letter's name printed on the page. One evening I told Mandy that we need to read *Dr. Seuss's ABC* book everyday and practice her letters and that soon she will be able to read. She said, "You mean I will be able to read all-by-myself?" I told her that she would if we really worked at it. Well, early the next morning while I was still in bed, Mandy brought me her *ABC Book* and wanted to read it! This was a good sign that Mandy was ready to begin some simple phonics instruction in a fun, non-stressed manner. (I've found many of the suggestions in *Games*

(I don't recommend this procedure for all children, but I mention it to emphasize that it is beneficial to use a child's interests to teach him basic skills.)

for Reading by Peggy Kaye are appropriate for Mandy at this stage.)

Mandy has recently reached the point where she loves to sit while I read to her. She doesn't have to busy herself *undoing* what someone else has just finished *doing*. She also enjoys *reading* to me. She will take a favorite book that is partially or completely memorized and *read* it to me. It is special when Mandy invents her own story to accompany the illustrations in a book. On a recent visit to the library, we saw three little girls about Mandy's age sitting at a small table. Mandy pulled up a chair and began *reading* them a story from a book she has not read or heard before. The little girls sat mesmerized as she wove her tale. Mandy had a captive audience and she loved it.

All of the processes I have mentioned are paving the way for Mandy to learn to really read. Let's review these pre-reading processes. First, when she was very young, Mandy played nearby while I read to the other children. Then as her attention span increased, she sat, looked, and listened (and commented) while I read to her. (Even when Mandy was an infant we read baby board books.) Then Mandy *read* to me and created her own stories. We have always made books available for her to freely look through, we have also always insisted that she have a respect for books and not destroy them. Now she is learning the names for the letters of the alphabet and the sounds they generally make.

Earlier this year, Mandy dictated and illustrated her first book entitled, **Brown Bear Gets Lost**. My four older children also made books during the same time period. Mandy was thrilled that she was actually making a real book, too. She had often looked at the books her siblings had previously made.

Mandy dictated her story to me over the course of three days. I initially wrote the story in longhand and then my daughter Melissa typed it into the computer. Each day Mandy made an illustration to be included in her book. I taught her to draw a bear by making a series of circles with her pencil. Then she colored her pictures. Once the illustrations were complete and the text was printed on the pages,

Mandy helped me glue the pages and sew the book binding. Afterward we made a book jacket which Mandy illustrated. This book jacket contains a front flap with information about the book and a back flap with information about the author/illustrator. My boys dictated the information for their book jacket flaps to me as I sat at the computer, and Mandy *typed* on another computer, listening to every word they uttered. (She was probably typing what they were saying.) Then it was Mandy's turn to dictate her passages to be used for her book jacket flaps. She was all excited about telling about herself as her brothers had done. She even understood, without my explanation, that the back jacket flap was to read as if someone other than the author had written it. She was copying or mimicking what she had heard her brothers say, and she was applying it to herself. (Children often do this while engaged in a pretend conversation on the telephone.) This is the passage she dictated to me concerning herself, the author/illustrator.

> *Mandy is three years old, and she likes to ride her bike, read books, and "type" on the computer. She loves hamsters and birds. Mandy likes bears and dolls, too. This is Mandy's first book, and she wants to write some more books soon.*

I then added, "Mandy is the youngest of five children." Well, I had typed what Mandy dictated, printed it, pasted it on the back inside flap of her book jacket, and she was *still* telling me all about herself! She then asked, "Mommy, did you get all that?" I explained that she would have to write an autobiography next!

Raymond, who turned eight years old this summer, made great progress in his reading abilities as we were making books. The children spent a week getting their basic stories written or dictated. As Raymond would dictate his story for his book, I would type it into the computer. Then each day we began with Raymond reading aloud the portion of his story that he had dictated to me the day before. The benefits of this were twofold as it served as a review of what Raymond had previously dictated, which enabled him to logically begin the next episode of his story, and it served as an enticing reader which kept his interest, challenged him sufficiently, but didn't overwhelm him. Once again, as I mentioned earlier when relaying a similar experience with my oldest son Robert, the student wasn't overburdened with deciphering and following a story line. Decoding was less difficult due to familiarity with the vocabulary, the child's own spoken vocabulary, and the story line was naturally interpreted as it was created by the child.

The benefits of this were twofold as it served as a review of what Raymond had previously dictated, which enabled him to logically begin the next episode of his story, and it served as an enticing reader which kept his interest, challenged him sufficiently, but didn't overwhelm him.

CHAPTER FOUR
NARRATION: **The Simple Yet Effective Method**
for Mastering Composition

NARRATION:
The Simple Yet Effective Method
for Mastering Composition

Some children, like my son Raymond, have a natural ability to tell stories. Raymond's difficulty usually lies in his inability to *end* a story. His imagination seems to run away with him. But, there are children who find it loathsome to develop a story of their own. This is where the narration method for mastering composition is extremely useful. Read a story to your child, have him orally narrate the story while you write it down, and then allow him to use his own version of the story as a reader. (You might find that you'll be more successful if you tape the narration and then transcribe it.)

As I explained in the previous chapter, the story flow and vocabulary are familiar, thus there is less difficulty with decoding than with an unfamiliar story.

This method also gives the child practice with developing a story without the burden of creating characters and plot. By this simple narration process, he makes the story his own.

I received a letter from a mother who used my book, ***Creating Books With Children***, to lead her children in making books. Her oldest child had no difficulty in developing a story, but her younger child was stumped as to what to write. I had mentioned that in devising a story, a child might retell a favorite Bible story. So this mother asked her son, "What's your favorite story?" He chose the story about David and Goliath. She proceeded to read him the story a few times, reading several different versions, and then she asked him to retell her the well-loved Bible story. As he dictated, the mother wrote her son's own words. This transcription became his story and he made illustrations to accompany it.

This simple process will probably contribute more toward building that child's future ability to read and write on his own than any number of teacher contrived worksheets.

Read a story to your child, have him orally narrate the story while you write it down, and then allow him to use his own version of the story as a reader.

By this simple narration process, he makes the story his own.

This simple process will probably contribute more toward building that child's future ability to read and write on his own than any number of teacher contrived worksheets.

Often a child can decode words far above his typical grade level, but cannot put a simple story in his own words or compose a few sentences representing his own thoughts.

Young children can successfully be encouraged to narrate storybooks containing lots of illustrations. After the story has been read, once or twice, the children can narrate the story by following the pictures. This helps them to keep events in their proper time sequence. Older children will also find this beneficial if they are having difficulty with narration.

Initially, if the older children's narration is based on a long book, have them narrate each chapter as it is read aloud. (The difficulty of the book to be narrated can be determined by the ability of the children to comprehend the story as it is read aloud.)

Later, written narration should be encouraged as well as oral narration of material that is read aloud. Sufficient practice with oral narration at a young age will greatly facilitate the ability of a child to give a written narration when he is older. It is important that oral narration be continued with older children, just as it is important that older children continue to participate in the family read-aloud time.

Because a child can read on his own, doesn't mean that he doesn't need to have stories read aloud to him. And following this same manner of thought, it doesn't mean that because he can write he should no longer participate in oral narration. Oral narration is also important in that it opens up the gate to discussion. And it is as we discuss our readings with our children, that thinking skills are developed. I'll elaborate further on the aspects of discussion in the next chapter.

Dinnertime can serve as an appropriate time for some narration exercises as a captive audience is already established. Children, and people in general tend to perform at a more proficient level if they have an audience. Let's face it, sometimes our children need to perform for someone other than just Mom.

I would like to give you an example of a successful dinnertime narration given by my daughter, Michelle, awhile ago. This narration came about in a rather spontaneous manner as she had recently finished reading an exciting book, and she just had to tell someone about it. The book she had just completed was Gary Paulsen's suspenseful novel, **Hatchet**. In this drama a young teenage boy is flying in a small plane to visit his father in Canada. The plane crashes after the pilot dies of a heart attack. The young boy manages to escape from the plane with only his hatchet secured to his belt. This hatchet was a going away gift from his mother. He manages to survive several weeks alone in the wilderness with the aid of his hatchet.

Michelle did a wonderful job of slowly unfolding the tale, enunciating each suspenseful episode as her siblings sat perched on the edges of their chairs. In turn, each would quickly ask her an important question hoping to resolve the current dilemma facing the main character. Michelle would very slowly answer this question with a "Well..." and then she would draw out her sentences, carefully choosing each word so as to keep her listeners enticed.

Michelle had an eager audience and took full advantage of this situation. I too was listening with strained ears and wide eyes as I cleaned up the after-dinner dishes in the kitchen. Michelle was surprised at the end of her performance when I announced that she had spent 50 minutes narrating the story. I was careful to log this as part of Michelle's schoolwork for the day under **Narration.** I also logged it as part of the other children's schoolwork under **Listening Comprehension.** They were listening and comprehending as was evident by their questions and their attentiveness.

Let me warn you that this practice of narration can be dangerous too. One day this past summer my son, Robert, was absorbed in a historical book about Egypt which specifically describes the processes of mummification. He was so interested in what he learned that he was eager to share this new found information. He wanted to narrate what he had read.

The problem was that his brother and two older sisters *did not* want to learn about mummification, and Robert was banished from

Let me warn you that this practice of narration can be dangerous too.

the family room. I was in the shower and my youngest child, Mandy, was sitting on my bed reading books to herself. Robert came in and found a willing subject.

Mandy was listening intently as Robert elaborated on the finer points of mummification. I walked into the room as Mandy was saying, "Yeah, then what did they do?" I knew that Robert had been reading about the mummies of Ancient Egypt when I left the room to take a shower, so I quickly asked him what he was telling Mandy. He confessed saying, "Well, she's the only one that would listen to me!" I nicely explained that you *don't* tell a four-year-old about mummies. And I was right, because every night thereafter for about two weeks, Mandy took refuge in our bed in the middle of the night. Remember, narration is a powerful tool, so use it wisely!

We have numerous Bible storybooks, Bible story audio cassettes, and even a few Bible story video cassettes. My youngest daughter, Mandy, now four years old, has fallen in love with one particular Bible storybook. Each day we read many stories from her book, and although we read a variety of stories, we must read and re-read and re-read several favorites.

Her three favorite stories are currently, "The Prodigal Son," "A Wise King" (about Solomon when he ordered that the dispute between the two women over the baby be settled by cutting the baby in half), and "David Fights a Giant."

One day I was conducting a **Creating Books with Children Workshop,** and upon entering the church where the workshop was held, Mandy immediately noticed a rather large painting of David slaying Goliath. She looked puzzled as she stared at the picture. Then she asked, "Why is David so small? He doesn't look like the David in my book." Now I could see the wheels turning inside her head. I tried to explain that each artist draws David and Goliath differently because we don't really know what they looked like. Then she wanted to know, "Is this a real story?"

I could guess that she was wondering that if this was a real story, then why weren't the pictures real. We talked about it some more, and for days she kept asking about the painting in the church. I got out several of our Bible storybooks and read her the story of David and Goliath from each book. She studied the various likenesses of the characters and criticized them as she knew fact from fiction.

Through this sequence of events, Mandy's world was broadened. She was really thinking about what she heard and what she saw. One of the Bible storybooks contains a very useful follow-up to each story. It includes individual pictures from the story, such as a picture of David, another of his sling, another of the brook, another of the stones, another of Goliath, another of Goliath's sword, and so forth.

Then the book asks the child to name each person or article. Following this game, they ask the child to retell the story in their own words. This is a terrific device for encouraging a child to narrate. The picture of each person and article helps to place those people and objects in the child's mind, so she is able to snatch them up while recalling the story.

This is a good narration technique that can be used with any picture book. Pictures are useful when a child retells a story as they help her to keep the sequence of events in proper order. Naming each character and article depicted before the narration is given helps the child to look for details as well. It makes the process of narration seem more like a game.

Mandy loves to offer her biblical knowledge at family Bible study time. One day my husband was discussing Galations with the children and he mentioned Paul. Immediately Mandy latched onto that name. She knew Paul, she met him in her Bible storybook. She then proceeded to tell her father, "Paul was blinded by a bright light!" He asked her a few questions which helped her to recount the entire story.

There have been several occasions when the mention of a person from the pages of Scripture has caused a light to turn on in Mandy's head, and she excitedly relates the story that she has learned about this person. She's pleased that she knows about the Bible

Through this sequence of events, Mandy's world was broadened.

Pictures are useful when a child retells a story as they help her to keep the sequence of events in proper order.

too, and that she can participate in the discussion.

Familiarity with a well-loved story can also offer an opportunity to extend a young child's attention span. The Bible storybook that Mandy has grown to love so well is very simple. Each story only spans two or three pages with large illustrations and large type. Mandy has memorized a number of stories and portions of several others. Her interest in the painting of David and Goliath in the church spurred questions which caused us to read the account of David's triumph in several other Bible storybooks offering longer narratives. Because she was acquainted with the story and took a special interest in it, she was ready to listen to a longer, more detailed version of that story. Now, she is anxious for me to read from these longer Bible storybooks, which didn't interest her earlier. She searches through the more lengthy stories, studying the illustrations, which are of course depicted differently from the pictures in her simple book. Once she locates a familiar picture, she asks, "Is this Jonah and the Big Fish?" or is this "The Prodigal Son?" Then I proceed to read her those stories. It has now become a game for her to cart in a number of Bible storybooks and find "Daniel in the Lion's Den," or "David and Goliath" in each book.

Older children may enjoy drawing pictures to accompany a story you are reading aloud. Then they can use their pictures to help them narrate the story to you. This is especially helpful for stories that have few or no illustrations accompanying them.

Children do not have to physically draw to paint pictures in their minds. You might read aloud a passage or two from a story you're sharing and ask what images come to mind as you speak. You can assist them with this activity by asking questions such as: "What do you think the man looked like?", "Can you describe the kitchen in the old farm house?", "What color do you think the big cat was?", and so forth.

As we read we form images in our minds, images that are very real to us. Besides describing a visual image with words, your children can describe the personalities and character traits of the individuals

As we read we form images in our minds, images that are very real to us.

in the story. This is less difficult if they describe how a person behaved in a particular segment of the story.

Another suggestion is to read a passage that is spoken by one of the characters from a book you've been reading aloud, without disclosing the character's identity. See if the children can guess which character is speaking. What makes them think that this particular character made that statement? We found this to be a fun game to play while reading **Little Women**, as each of the four March sisters have very distinctive personalities. We noticed that it is easy to detect a passage spoken by Jo, as she has such bold mannerisms. And conversely, Beth's patient, kind disposition is clearly evident in her dialogue.

For more ideas on teaching narration and composition while integrating grammar studies, see Karen Andreola's text, **Simply Grammar**, grades 4 - 8. **English for the Thoughtful Child**, by Cyndy Shearer incorporates these same teaching techniques geared for the primary grades.

CHAPTER FIVE
Reading Broadens Our World

Reading Broadens Our World

The parameters of our world and those of our children are broadened as we read aloud with them and as they advance in their own readings. It is exciting to be able to take what has been read and relate it to our own lives.

The children take an active part in reading as they listen, discuss, narrate, read aloud, or write about a book or a segment of a book that has been shared by the family. They're encouraged to be a part of several aspects relating to reading, not only reading itself.

Love and enthusiasm for reading is nurtured as the children begin to see parallels between the different books they read, or listen to being read. For example, I have read *The Dangerous Journey*, a retelling of Bunyan's, *Pilgrim's Progress* with my boys twice. My husband read it aloud to all the children once. My daughter, Melissa, read it aloud to the boys, and Robert read it to himself.

This all occurred over the course of perhaps two years. It is a well-loved book, and even my younger son, Raymond, has read parts of it to himself, primarily enjoying the incredible illustrations. This particular version of *Pilgrim's Progress* uses portions of the original text, carefully chosen by Oliver Hunkin and wonderfully illustrated by Alan Parry.

Recently at a home school curriculum fair, we bought another adaptation of Bunyan's, *Pilgrim's Progress* for children entitled, *The Evergreen Wood*, retold by Linda Parry and illustrated by her husband, Alan Parry. (Mr. Parry also illustrated *Dangerous Journey*.) This is a somewhat simpler version than *Dangerous Journey*, but it is also expertly written and illustrated.

I read this rendering of *Pilgrim's Progress* aloud to my boys over the course of two or three days. I was thoroughly pleased with their enthusiasm over the story. Without any prompting from me, they were continuously comparing the two adaptations of Bunyan's classic story.

It is exciting to be able to take what has been read and relate it to our own lives.

Love and enthusiasm for reading is nurtured as the children begin to see parallels between the different books they read, or listen to being read.

Dangerous Journey more closely depicts the original work, while *The Evergreen Wood* is based on the pilgrimage of Christopher Mouse. Therefore, the characters in the latter version are depicted as mice, rats, a cat, an owl, a fox, a badger, a frog, a lamb, and so forth.

Robert and Raymond loved to tell me which of the creatures in *The Evergreen Wood* paralleled the characters in *Dangerous Journey*. One of the boys would say, for example, "Oh, Mom, you know who the two tethered owls in *The Evergreen Wood* represent, don't you?" And as I tried desperately to remember, he would excitedly tell me, "You remember, they're like the two chained lions at the lodge in *Dangerous Journey*. "Oh yes, of course I remember, now that you've refreshed my memory," I replied.

They couldn't wait for me to read further from *The Evergreen Wood* so that they could discover which creatures, places, and events represented or paralleled the characters, places, and events in *Dangerous Journey*.

Now, as if this wasn't enough excitement to see parallels in two books we had read aloud together, we unexpectedly stumbled upon still another story whose underlying theme was based on Bunyan's classic.

The next book we selected to read after *The Evergreen Wood* was Louisa May Alcott's, *Little Women*. (I had previously read *Little Men* to the boys and we decided we should back up and read *Little Women*. Oops!)

My girls had read these books independently, so I didn't get the benefit of reading them aloud beforehand. Unfortunately, they had read an abridged version of *Little Women*, so now I'm reading the original with them, too.

Now as we embarked on our reading of *Little Women*, we were greeted with the preface which was adapted from John Bunyan's, *Pilgrim's Progress*. The significance of this entry didn't come to me until we read the first chapter, "Playing Pilgrims."

This first scene opens with the girls lamenting over the dismal

Now, as if this wasn't enough excitement to see parallels in two books we had read aloud together, we unexpectedly stumbled upon still another story whose underlying theme was based on Bunyan's classic.

reality that their Christmas was going to be a poor one.

You know the reason mother proposed not having any presents this Christmas was because it is going to be a hard winter for everyone; and she thinks we ought not to spend money for pleasure, when our men are suffering so in the army.[2]

The four March girls continued to grumble over their circumstance, each showing a very self-centered side of their character.

The dialogue continues in this manner for awhile when the girls are suddenly brought back to their senses by the striking of the clock. Soon their mother would be home. They decided then to spend the small amount of money they each possessed on their beloved mother.

After supper Mother read the letter she received from Father, who entered into the military as a chaplain during the strife-torn Civil War years.

Give them all my dear love and a kiss. Tell them I think of them by day, pray for them by night, and find my best comfort in their affection at all times. A year seems very long to wait before I see them, but remind them that while we wait we may all work, so that these hard days need not be wasted. I know they will remember all I said to them, that they will be loving children to you, will do their duty faithfully, fight their bosom enemies bravely, and conquer themselves so beautifully, that when I come back to them I may be fonder and prouder than ever of my little women.[3]

Following this touching letter, the girls each expressed shame for their selfish attitudes and resolved to be better so as not to disappoint their father.

Mrs. March broke the silence that followed Jo's words, by saying in her cheery voice, "Do you remember how you used to play Pilgrim's Progress when you were little things? Nothing delighted you more than to have me tie my piece-bags on your

*backs for burdens, give you hats and sticks and rolls of paper,
and let you travel through the house from the cellar, which was
the City of Destruction, up, up, to the house-top, where you
had all the lovely things you could collect to make a Celestial
City."* [4]

Each girl related her favorite part of the game. Then the girls'
mother remarked:

*We never are too old for this, my dear, because it is a play
we are playing all the time in one way or another. Our burdens
are here, our road is before us, and the longing for goodness
and happiness is the guide that leads us through many troubles
and mistakes to the peace which is a true Celestial City. Now,
my little pilgrims, suppose you begin again, not in play, but in
earnest, and see how far on you can get before father comes
home.* [5]

The mother went on to explain that the girl's bundles were the
burdens that each was carrying now.

*"We were in the slough of despond tonight, and Mother
came and pulled us out as Help did in the book. We ought to
have our roll of directions, like Christian. What shall we do
about that?" asked Jo, delighted with the fancy which lent a
little romance to the very dull task of doing her duty."*

*"Look under your pillows, Christmas morning, and you
will find your guide-book," replied Mrs. March.* [6]

Chapter two begins with Jo waking in the gray dawn of Christmas
morning feeling a sense of disappointment.

*Then she remembered her mother's promise, and slipping
her hand under her pillow, drew out a little crimson-covered
book. She knew it very well, for it was that beautiful old story
of the best life ever lived, and Jo felt that it was a true guide-
book for any pilgrim going the long journey.* [7]

The four girls each received their guidebooks and decided to
read a little each morning as soon as they awakened.

After reading these chapters, Robert and Raymond decided it

would be fun to play Pilgrim's Progress at our house. They announced that the garage would make a suitable City of Destruction as its present condition lends itself well to that descriptive title, and their loft bedroom would be a satisfactory Celestial City as it is the loftiest (excuse the pun) point within the house. The boys remarked that they would let their bundles or burdens drop from their backs as they ascended the ladder to the Celestial City as the March girls had let their bundles totter down the stairs in **Little Women**. They went on enthusiastically describing how they would play Pilgrim's Progress in our home.

Let's review the significance of the knowledge my boys and I gained through reading three books with an overlapping theme. First, we read **Dangerous Journey** and my children expressed their understanding of this classic tale by paralleling it to Scripture. As Oliver Hunkin states in the introduction to **Dangerous Journey**:

> **"But rapidly the fame of Bunyan grew, and his work has become recognized by millions of readers not as an idle tale at all, but as a story with a hidden meaning -- an 'allegory' of that Dangerous Journey, which is, in fact, the journey of Everyman from this world to the next."**

After several readings of this version of Bunyan's classic tale, we later read a younger child's rendering of this story called, **The Evergreen Wood**. The boys were paralleling the details of this version with those of **Dangerous Journey**. And thirdly we read **Little Women** in which we were given a more realistic glimpse of the journey of the pilgrim as played out by the March sisters. This journey was revealed to us through their present trials and in a more humorous tone as we learned how the March sisters had played Pilgrim's Progress as young children. (Additional references are made to the Pilgrim's journey throughout **Little Women**.) It is interesting to note that the author of **Little Women**, Louisa May Alcott, assumed that her readers were familiar with Bunyan's, **Pilgrim's Progress**.

My girls also joined in our Pilgrim's Progress Unit Study. As literary and handwriting exercises, they copied or took from dictation on

After reading these chapters, Robert and Raymond decided it would be fun to play Pilgrim's Progress at our house.

alternate days, the text of **Dangerous Journey**. Difficult words were researched, and we discussed their meanings. The girls also read **The Evergreen Wood** and made a list of the creatures in this narrative and the characters they parallel in **Dangerous Journey**.

The boys copied the text from **The Evergreen Wood**. I would write out the selection for them to copy the night before. Sometimes I would write the passage, skipping lines which enabled them to write directly below my writing. On other days, they would copy directly from a separate sheet of paper on which I had neatly copied the passage. And every few days I would personally dictate that day's passage to them. After they copied their selection for the day, they read it aloud to me individually, and then we discussed it. I also drew spelling words from these passages, and the boys typed the chosen words three times each on the computer. I gave assistance if they needed it, explaining various rules as we proceeded, such as changing the *y* to *i* before adding a suffix as in the word *tried*. I also brought out phonetic rules such as *aw* as in *hawk*. (**The Natural Speller**, by Kathryn Stout will prove beneficial for brushing up on all those spelling rules!)

Typing the spelling words gave the boys' hands a break from writing and allowed them to practice their keyboard skills. It also enabled me to evaluate their typing abilities during this activity, making certain they were using the correct key strokes. (We have a computer typing program that the children use frequently.) Each day we printed their spelling lists to keep in their folders with their copying exercises.

As we read through **Little Women** we discussed the allusions made to the **Pilgrim's Progress** story, which were even more evident as all the children had been copying from an adaptation of this timeless classic. We found it interesting to note that more copies of Bunyan's original, **Pilgrim's Progress** have been printed in history than any other book with the exception of the Bible.

The children each decided to make a **Pilgrim's Progress** game. In the front of both **Dangerous Journey** and **The Evergreen Wood**,

Typing the spelling words gave the boys' hands a break from writing and allowed them to practice their keyboard skills.

appears a map of the country through which Christian, or Christopher Mouse, must travel. These maps reminded my son, Raymond, of a game board, and so the idea of making a game came to life.

Making games to accompany a unit study is an extremely valuable project. When using textbooks, children are often required to answer questions at the end of the chapter. When designing a game, children are required to not only answer questions, but they must also make up the questions. This requires much effort as they must search for facts and accurately formulate a question.

Index cards, posterboard, and dice are often all that is necessary to make fun and interesting games. The game cards can contain questions pertaining directly to the study as well as include material to liven up the game. This may include cards indicating, for example, that the player must go back a designated number of spaces, or that the player may roll again. So, some cards are included just for fun, to add adventure to the game, while others ask factual information pertaining to the study.

I generally suggest that my children make up twenty-five question cards and ten additional cards. Then they write the rules for their games. It is obvious to see that there is a great deal that can be learned during the game making process, and the unit study material is easily reviewed through playing the games.

After spending several weeks copying from **Dangerous Journey** and **The Evergreen Wood**, we began reading from the original version of Bunyan's **Pilgrim's Progress**, which contains unusual grammatical structure and difficult vocabulary. Because we had first read the two adaptations of this wonderful story, we were better able to follow the original version. It is full of treasures and offers much material for meaningful discussion. Many allusions are made to biblical characters, and even little Mandy picked up on this as she listened while playing at my feet.

It was obvious that my children took pleasure in being able to participate in a discussion of **Pilgrim's Progress**, because they had some previous knowledge of the subject from which to draw. *Reading*

Making games to accompany a unit study is an extremely valuable project.

It is obvious to see that there is a great deal that can be learned during the game making process, and the unit study material is easily reviewed through playing the games.

Breadth in our reading helps us to see relationships, develop concepts, and apply knowledge.

broadens our world. This holds true whether we are reading the newspaper, a magazine, a novel, a picture book, a poetry book, a history book, a science book, or any number of different kinds of worthy books.

Breadth in our reading helps us to see relationships, develop concepts, and apply knowledge.

CHAPTER SIX
Where to Find Good, Worthy Books

Where to Find Good, Worthy Books

Many parents realize the need to provide their children with good books. Even more importantly, good books should be read aloud to the children. But finding these worthy books may present a problem, especially since there exists such an overabundance of unworthy books. These unworthy books range from time wasters to those harmful in content.

I'm going to gladly recommend a number of excellent guides to excellent books. I'm not suggesting you buy and read all of these books initially, but that you choose one or two, read them, use them, and six months or so later, choose another book or two to read and use. Continue this process until you've read all or most all of these books. I often meet with zealous homeschooling parents who buy numerous books at a curriculum fair only to find that when the next year's fair comes around, they've still not read the previously purchased books. A better method is to limit your purchasing and to increase your reading and utilizing of good books. A book that is read, re-read, highlighted, filled with notes and referred to often is far more beneficial than ten wonderful books that sit on your shelf gathering dust. This holds true for all curriculum materials whether they are geared for the parents or the children.

Owning a plethora of quality educational materials will not benefit our children unless they utilize them, and you can only use so many items effectively at one time. So don't fret if your budget doesn't allow you to purchase all those wonderful materials you want for your children. Limit your purchases and increase the use of those few purchases. Let the children saturate themselves in a given area for a given time.

I make it a point to only buy enough materials for one or two unit studies at a time. Once these studies have been completed, I plan for only one or two more. In this manner I do not overwhelm myself, and I'm free to be sensitive to the Lord's leading in another

A book that is read, re-read, highlighted, filled with notes and referred to often is far more beneficial than ten wonderful books that sit on your shelf gathering dust.

Limit your purchases and increase the use of those few purchases.

It is also beneficial for your children to see that you read, study, and grow in wisdom and knowledge.

Books are experiences that make us grow, that add something to our inner stature.[8]

direction if necessary. I'm not locked into a schedule for the year that can't flex to meet the needs of my family and to follow the direction of the Lord.

I don't mean to sound as if I'm giving orders or a class assignment, but I know what a blessing each of these books I'm about to recommend has been to me and my family. It is also beneficial for your children to see that you read, study, and grow in wisdom and knowledge.

The first book I would like to suggest is **Honey for a Child's Heart**. This book is first in line as it is full of encouragement and ideas for developing a read-aloud-habit in the home. It also contains references to specific books for children categorized by age group.

As the author of **Honey for a Child's Heart**, Gladys Hunt states:

> **That is what a book does. It introduces us to people and places we wouldn't ordinarily know. A good book is a magic gateway into a wider world of wonder, beauty, delight, and adventure. Books are experiences that make us grow, that add something to our inner stature.**[8]

As I stated in the last chapter, reading broadens our world. Secondly, I am pleased to suggest **Books Children Love: A Guide to the Best Children's Literature**, by Elizabeth Wilson.

Mrs. Wilson has carefully arranged books listed into categories such as Art and Architecture, Bible/Spiritual Teaching, Biography, Crafts, Dance/Drama, Geography and History, Language, Literature, Mathematics, Music, Physical Education, Reference and Research, Science and more! Each book listing includes the complete title, author, publisher, year published, number of pages, and approximate grade level.

Each book also receives a one paragraph description of its contents. Many books fall into more than one category, and therefore they are cross-referenced to those additional listings. **Books Children Love** is a terrific resource and a valuable timesaving reference book. Books for pleasurable reading or reading pertaining to a topic of study are easily found.

My daughter, Melissa, now 12 years old, has been using this guide for several years to locate enjoyable books for herself and her siblings. We call her our family librarian as she reads numerous commentaries on books, searching for appealing books for the other children. She makes a list containing book titles and authors and takes it when we visit the library. She's had fairly good success locating the desired books, and her brothers and sisters are usually excited over the selections she makes for them.

Melissa is a doll collector and loves to read all kinds of books about dolls. By using various book guides and making inquiries into the library's computer, she has located many and varied books on dolls. Through her diligence, she has also been able to locate unreferenced books about dolls by thoroughly reading the books she has been able to obtain. She has found that information about additional books on her topic of interest are located in front and/or back jacket flaps, in prefaces, introductions, forwards, and in bibliographies.

Failing to completely read a book may mean leaving a treasure buried for a more inquisitive explorer. Melissa has cultivated her love for reading into a love for researching. Although her research seems to be in a pleasure-related area, the skills she has acquired can be transferred to any field of study.

Thirdly, I would like to recommend that parents read, **A Family Program for Reading Aloud**, developed by Rosalie June Slater. The information contained in this guide includes: The Purpose and Importance of a Family Program, Skills Needed in Reading Aloud, Books to Read to Younger Children, Introducing America in Your Reading Aloud, Evaluating Your Family Interests Through Reading in Depth, and Restoring Heroes and Heroines to our Reading Aloud.

Excellent material is included for the study of a select group of authors such as: Charles Dickens, Sir Walter Scott, Washington Irving, Nathaniel Hawthorne, Anne Bradstreet, Marguerite Henry, and others. A significant portion of the book is also donated to the study of America through the reading of biographies of great men and

Failing to completely read a book may mean leaving a treasure buried for a more inquisitive explorer. … Although her research seems to be in a pleasure-related area, the skills she has acquired can be transferred to any field of study.

women. This guide is published by the Foundation for American Christian Education, and it contains rich information useful for conducting meaningful unit studies.

Fourthly, I would like to suggest a wonderful book that I recently read entitled, **Let the Authors Speak** by Carolyn Hatcher. This book is subtitled: **A Guide to Worthy Books Based on Historical Setting**. Mrs. Hatcher also includes pertinent information on the importance and process of narration. She emphasizes that parents do not need to be educational experts, only guides. Mrs. Hatcher states:

> **I'm not sure how anyone else will react to this idea, but it certainly removed a burden from my shoulders knowing that to give my children the best I only needed to be a guide to the best.**[9]

And lastly I'd like to encourage you to read, **Read for Your Life: Turning Teens into Readers**. This book was written by the author of **Honey for a Child's Heart**, Gladys Hunt, along with Barbara Hampton. Not only does this guide contain more than 300 books reviewed by Barbara Hampton, but it includes inspirations from Gladys Hunt on how to read a book, what makes a good book, and how to distinguish between good, better, and best. This book offers a truly delightful literature course for teens and parents. If you thought literature was boring in high school, you're in for a surprise!

You may be saying to yourself, this woman is crazy to suggest I read five books, all guides to the best in literature. Remember, I didn't say to read them all at once. Read one of the books, familiarize yourself with it, and really use it! This will be far more beneficial than trying to scan each book briefly and never getting thoroughly acquainted with any of them. Later, as time and finances permit, choose another of these excellent guides and immerse yourself in it.

Each author is an expert in conveying her thoughts from her viewpoint. Each brings to light different ideas, suitable for certain people, at certain times, under certain circumstances. We are truly blessed to have at our disposal the insights of these gifted women. Each of these guides contributes to "Honey for a Mother's Heart."

When you continue to study and learn, you offer your children a special example, an example that says, as Charlotte Mason put it, "Education is a Life."

When you continue to study and learn, you offer your children a special example, an example that says, as Charlotte Mason put it, "Education is a Life."

CHAPTER SEVEN
Taking What We Read to Heart

Taking What We Read to Heart

As we conduct our unit studies or spend time just reading enjoyable books together, there inevitably springs up some gem, some delightful morsel that is worthy of our contemplation. My desire is to memorize some of these gems, but too often this is a difficult task as we tend to devour so many excellent books in such a condensed period of time.

While studying poetry and poets, we decided to investigate Robert Louis Stevenson. Not only were we enchanted by his poems, but we stumbled over such a gem as I previously described. Mr. Stevenson said that wherever he went, he took two books with him, "one to read and one to write in."

I figured that he must use that writing book for putting down thoughts that came to him so that they didn't slip away. But after thinking about it for awhile, I deduced that perhaps he also used that writing book to record passages, gems as it were, from the books he was currently reading. This gave me an idea. We should keep a **Food for Thought Book** or a **Reader's Journal**. Often in book stores you will see beautifully decorated blank journals of all types, some with no titles, and others that say **Mother's Journal**, **Author's Journal**, and so on.

Often times I'm stumped when I try to recall a particular book. Reading so widely makes it difficult to remember where we read *what* and exactly *how* the author constructed the thought. A **Reader's Journal** solves this dilemma and provides a good literary exercise.

As we copy pertinent passages from works that we read, we become intimately acquainted with the authors and receive the benefit of their ideas and literary expertise. This is why copying good writing is such a fine tool for learning to write well. It's a very simple practice, yet very effective. Because it is so uncomplicated a task, its effectiveness is multiplied as it enables us to perform it on a regular

*Reading so widely makes it difficult to remember where we read **what** and exactly **how** the author constructed the thought.*

As we copy pertinent passages from works that we read, we become intimately acquainted with the authors and receive the benefit of their ideas and literary expertise.

basis. If we are able to follow through with something consistently, it becomes habit; if it becomes habit, it becomes a part of who we are.

It is important to implement this habit of copying worthy excerpts, or gems, from the books we read. These literary passages to be copied, whether from history, science, novels, classics, poetry, and so on become the focus of our studies. This eliminates the need for dry workbook exercises and offers a richer, more meaningful dimension to our studies. While copying a passage, or taking that passage from dictation, many elements come into play. We must focus on spelling, punctuation, and grammatical structure.

Another benefit of this process of copying significant excerpts from books we read is that it stimulates discussion. It enables us to take a closer look at what the author is saying. It also allows us a means to compare one book or idea to another book or idea. It strengthens our observation skills as we search for gems to add to our *Reader's Journal*.

Hopefully, the incorporation of a ***Reader's Journal*** in our academic pursuits with our children will encourage them to keep such a journal for excerpts taken from books they read on their own. Of course, some books don't lend themselves to this sort of activity, especially humorous books or books for young children. But as the reader matures, he should be reading more and more books with gems worthy of notation. Even humorous books may fall into this category as everyone needs a good laugh from time to time.

It strengthens our observation skills as we search for gems to add to our **Reader's Journal**.

CHAPTER EIGHT
*Ideas for Implementing a Reader's Journal
in Our Children's Daily Schoolwork*

Ideas for Implementing a Reader's Journal in Our Children's Daily Schoolwork

As I mentioned in the last chapter, if we instill the habit of developing a **Reader's Journal** based on books we read together as a family, our children may be motivated to keep a **Reader's Journal** based on books they read for personal enjoyment.

I would like to offer a sampling of excerpts I chose to include in our **Reader's Journal** when we studied sign language. We read numerous books during the course of this study, and one of our favorites was **The Story of My Life**, by Helen Keller.

Each night I pre-read the chapter I planned to read aloud to my children the next day. (No, I didn't spend days and weeks preparing ahead of time.) As I read the chapter, I searched for a valuable passage, a gem, to include in our **Reader's Journals**. Usually, this passage jumped out at me as it contained valuable information or insights that I deemed worthy of notation. Often this passage exemplified some character trait that I wanted to impress upon my children.

I would like to relate some background information drawing from Helen Keller's autobiography. Before Anne Sullivan came to teach Helen, her life was marred by darkness, darkness brought on by deafness and blindness. After her teacher came, she felt as if a veil of oppression had been lifted from her life.

As Helen explains in her autobiography:

Thus I came up out of Egypt and stood before Sinai, and a power divine touched my spirit and gave it sight, so that I beheld many wonders. And from the sacred mountain I heard a voice which said, "Knowledge is love and light and vision."[10]

As we read through Helen's autobiography, we noted the numerous references to biblical passages or events. These made excellent excerpts for inclusion in our **Reader's Journals** and offered research exercises as we sought to locate these references in the Bible.

Each night I pre-read the chapter I planned to read aloud to my children the next day.

Often this passage exemplified some character trait that I wanted to impress upon my children.

One of my favorite passages from *The Story of My Life* recounts how the mystery of language was first conveyed to Helen. Until this time, finger spelling was only a game to Helen; she didn't realize everything had a name.

We walked down the path to the well-house, attracted by the fragrance of the honeysuckle with which it was covered. Someone was drawing water and my teacher placed my hand under the spout. As the cool stream gushed over one hand she spelled into the other the word "water", first slowly, then rapidly. I stood still, my whole attention fixed upon the motions of her fingers. Suddenly I felt a misty consciousness as of something forgotten — a thrill of returning thought; and somehow the mystery of language was revealed to me. I knew then that "w-a-t-e-r" meant the wonderful cool something that was flowing over my hand. That living word awakened my soul, gave it light, hope, joy, set it free! There were barriers still, it is true, but barriers that could in time be swept away.[11]

Following this passage was another passage offering biblical inference.

I learned a great many new words that day. I do not remember what they all were; but I do know that "mother," "father," "sister," "teacher" were among them -- words that were to make the world blossom for me, "like Aaron's rod, with flowers."[12]

If we do not know the story of the departure of the children of Israel from Egypt and the miracle of Aaron's rod, these words of Helen's will have no meaning for us.

The following selections are remarks Helen made about the Bible.

I began to read the Bible long before I could understand it. Now it seems strange to me that there should have been a time when my spirit was deaf to its wondrous harmonies...

But how shall I speak of the glories I have since discovered in the Bible? For years I have read it with an ever-broadening sense of joy and inspiration; and I love it as I love no other book.

The Bible gives me a deep, comforting sense that "things seen are temporal, and things unseen are eternal."[13]

Helen's account of her experience at the well-house offers several avenues for discussion. What words does Helen use to describe the bower enveloping the well-house? What sensations did she feel as the water flowed over her hand? How did she feel after the "mystery of language had been revealed" to her? Realizing that Helen was both deaf and blind will help us to understand her perception of the incident.

Before reading the ***Story of My Life***, by Helen Keller, we read a biography about Thomas Hopkins Gallaudet who pioneered education for the deaf in America. This wonderful biography, which is now out of print but still available in many public libraries, is entitled, ***Gallaudet, Friend of the Deaf***, by Etta DeGering. (Another excellent, but less inspiring biography about Gallaudet that is currently in print is titled, ***A Deaf Child Listened***, by Anne Neimark.) Using either of these biographies, it is interesting to note comparisons between the teaching methods employed by Gallaudet and those used by Anne Sullivan to teach Helen Keller.

Gallaudet's first experience with teaching the deaf was when he taught his neighbor, little Alice Cogswell, that "h-a-t" written in the sand represented the hat he held in his hand. A beneficial exercise is to compare this incident with Helen's revelation of language at the well-house.

The following excerpt is from ***Gallaudet, Friend of the Deaf***, by Etta DeGering. First, I will fill in a little background information. Thomas Gallaudet is home for a visit from Andover Theological Seminary and is sitting on his front porch watching his brothers and sisters playing with the neighborhood children.

He called Theodore, his nine-year-old brother, from the circle. "Who is the little girl sitting over there by herself?"

Teddy looked in the direction he indicated. "Her? Why,

Helen's account of her experience at the well-house offers several avenues for discussion.

don't you know? She's Alice Cogswell. Doc Cogswell's girl --
lives next door."

"Why doesn't she play with the group?"

Teddy shrugged. "She can't. She's deaf and dumb."
Deaf and dumb. So that was it. "Bring her to me. Maybe I can
think of a game she can play. She looks lonesome."

Teddy ran over to Alice, made a sweeping motion "to
come," left her with Thomas, and hurried back to the circle.

Thomas smiled and patted the step beside him. Alice sat
on the very edge like a pink butterfly — if there are pink
butterflies — ready to take flight.

Now what? His granny story was of no use here. College
B.A. and M.A. degrees offered no solution. He thought fast.
With all his soul Thomas longed to open this child's "silent
prison," find a way for her to be one with the other children.
Her need was some way of conversing. Could she be taught to
write, he wondered.

Picking up his hat, the only thing he had at hand, he gave
it to her, and stooping, wrote "hat" in the sand of the path.

Alice looked at him blankly. The marks in the sand meant
nothing to her. Again and again, Thomas handed her the hat
and wrote "hat" in the sand. He pointed to the writing and
then to other things and shook his head. He pointed to the hat
and nodded vigorously.

Her forehead puckered. She was trying to understand. She
looked from the hat to the writing. What did those marks in the
sand have to do with the thing she held in her hand?

Thomas breathed a prayer.

Finally a glimmer of light shone in the hazel eyes. Her
forehead smoothed. She smiled and nodded.

For the first time in her life, Alice understood that things
had names, names that could be written in the sand.[14]

We can also note other similarities between these two life stories,
such as the circumstances surrounding Alice Cogswell's deafness and

the deafness of Helen Keller.

It may take the children several days to transcribe such a lengthy passage as the one I excerpted from **Gallaudet, Friend of the Deaf**, into their **Reader's Journals**. Younger children may write from dictation or copy only one or two key sentences from the passage, although the entire passage is re-read to them. (Passages are copied or taken from dictation after the selection has been read aloud.)

For instance, they may copy, "Again and again, Thomas handed her the hat and wrote 'hat' in the sand."

Phonics rules that appear in the words in the copied sentence can be circled and discussed. The children can write additional words that rhyme with *hat*. They may even wish to draw a hat to accompany their sentence. The *ed* ending such as in *handed* can be explained. Even young children can learn to capitalize the first word of a sentence and the names of people. Explain that most sentences end in a period. The commas and quotation marks may prove to be too difficult for young children at this point, but they can be made aware of them and their purposes without expecting mastery at this level.

We can learn much about effective writing by reading Helen's own words, as she causes us to see the world in a new light. Helen beckons us to use all of our senses to express our thoughts, just as she employed all of her functioning senses to produce descriptive narratives. As you read various selections from her writings, try to note which senses evoked the choice of words she used to convey her message.

The following passage offers a superb exercise in observation and description techniques. Helen has been recently left high in a tree by her teacher who thought her quite safe for a few moments while she went to prepare a picnic for them to enjoy from this lofty position.

Suddenly a change passed over the tree. All the sun's warmth left the air. I knew the sky was black, because all the heat, which meant light to me, had died out of the atmosphere. A strange odour came up from the earth. I knew it, it was the

Younger children may write from dictation or copy only one or two key sentences from the passage.

The commas and quotation marks may prove to be too difficult for young children at this point, but they can be made aware of them and their purposes without expecting mastery at this level.

odour that always precedes a thunderstorm, and a nameless fear clutched at my heart. I felt absolutely alone, cut off from my friends and the firm earth. The immense, the unknown, enfolded me. I remained still and expectant; a chilling terror crept over me. I longed for my teacher's return; but above all things I wanted to get down from that tree.

There was a moment of sinister silence, then a multitudinous stirring of the leaves. A shiver ran through the tree, and the wind sent forth a blast that would have knocked me off had I not clung to the branch with might and main. The tree swayed and strained. The small twigs snapped and fell about me in showers. A wild impulse to jump seized me, but terror held me fast. I crouched down in the fork of the tree. The branches lashed about me. I felt the intermittent jarring that came now and then, as if something heavy had fallen and the shock had traveled up till it reached the limb I sat on. It worked my suspense up to the highest point, and just as I was thinking the tree and I should fall together, my teacher seized my hand and helped me down. I clung to her, trembling with joy to feel the earth under my feet once more.[15]

What a gripping account this blind and deaf woman has related through the use of well chosen words! She causes us to feel her desperation, tremble along with her, and then almost collapse with relief once security has been attained. Much oral discussion can ensue from this suspenseful account. How did Helen know a storm was approaching? Describe each warning of the upcoming storm as Helen perceived them. Describe Helen's terror, what sensations did she feel during the storm? Relate the security she felt as she was rescued by her teacher.

Older children can copy the passage or write it as it is dictated to them. (Longer passages, such as this account of Helen's trial in the storm-tossed tree, may require more than one day to copy or write from dictation. Naturally, copying is a less difficult activity than writing a passage from dictation. This technique can be used by children who find dictation laborious. Often, if the passage to be studied is above my girls' dictation level, containing difficult vocabulary and/or punctuation, I allow them to copy the selection directly from the book.)

I like to tape record passages beforehand for my older girls to take from dictation to include in their **Reader's Journals**. As I slowly read the passage onto the tape, I add in uncertain punctuation. Long sentences may contain numerous commas and semicolons which the ear is not always able to discern. If I feel there is a word that might be difficult to spell, I read the entire sentence containing the word, and then I pause and spell the word. This gives them an opportunity to spell it themselves first and correct the spelling if they have made an error. I feel it is more important that the children write the correct spelling with my assistance rather than make a futile guess and reinforce a negative spelling. This also holds true for punctuation. As the children become more proficient in their writing, I omit some of these helps.

I like to tape record passages beforehand for my older girls to take from dictation to include in their **Reader's Journals**.

Numerous writing activities can center around the pertinent passages taken from the books we read in the course of our studies. For example, on one day they may copy or take the selection from dictation. On the next day, they may rewrite the passage in their own words or with the help of a thesaurus. They may write the definitions for specific words from the selection, being sure to choose the definitions that best suit the meanings as used in the context of the passage. They can rewrite the passage in another tense or as if related from another individual's perspective. For example, the incident with Helen in the storm-tossed tree could be rewritten from her teacher's point of view, or with a good dose of imagination, from the tree's perspective!

Numerous writing activities can center around the pertinent passages taken from the books we read in the course of our studies.

Younger children may copy a portion of the passage that you have neatly written out for them. I write a selection to be copied on lined paper, skipping every other line as I proceed, so that the children can write directly under my writing. I pay close attention to letter formation, size, and spacing. Although the younger children may only copy a sentence or two from the passage of study, they can listen carefully to the re-reading of the entire passage and participate in oral discussion pertaining to the selection. Many excerpts, such as this particular one relating Helen's frightful episode in the tree, also make excellent sketches for the children to pantomime or act out. Younger children especially enjoy this activity.

We also find it advantageous to select a simpler biography about the individual that we are studying. This shorter, less detailed biography offers an overview as the capable children read it aloud to the younger children. It also provides them practice with their oral presentation skills. Sometimes these less difficult biographical sketches offer suitable material for the younger children to copy. I try to locate a passage from the simpler biography that parallels the passage from the more detailed biography that we are implementing in our literary exercises. While conducting our Sign Language Unit Study, we chose a simple biography of Helen Keller to use along with her autobiography entitled, **A Picture Book of Helen Keller**, by David A. Adler.

It is easy to see that the benefits of a **Reader's Journal** are far reaching. The passages copied or taken from dictation offer a variety of literary exercises relating directly to the children's topic of study. (I know that I have personally benefited from them as well!) Time is not usurped by tedious, irrelevant, fill-in-the-blank workbook assignments. These exercises based on excerpts from our reading encourage the children to become more observant and more critical of what they read. Furthermore, capitalization, spelling, punctuation, sentence structure, and grammar can effectively be taught through copying and dictation exercises as well. This concept is succinctly expressed in **The Elements of Grammar**, by Margaret Shertzer.

In order to use English correctly and gracefully, it is necessary to recognize and practice using good grammar. Listening to speakers who are accustomed to speaking grammatically helps to train the ear to recognize correct usage. Good habits of speech will improve one's writing, but the

These exercises based on excerpts from our reading encourage the children to become more observant and more critical of what they read.

best training may be to read examples of effective writing.[16]

I believe that reading effective writing is essential to improving one's writing, as Margaret Shertzer affirms, but I believe that copying and taking from dictation samples of effective writing will further enhance writing abilities.

If you are questioning this teaching method of copying and dictation, you will find useful suggestions in Ruth Beechick's information packed book, ***You Can Teach Your Child Successfully***. For those desiring further assistance, I recommend using the ***Learning Language Arts Through Literature*** series to help acquaint you with this teaching method.

Excellent exercises and activities are developed based on passages taken from fine literature. After utilizing this material for a while, you will be able to integrate the teaching strategies incorporated in the ***Learning Language Arts Through Literature*** series with selections you have chosen relating to your unit of study.

A plan such as the following may work for you. Have your children spend five weeks, or so, conducting a Basic Skills Unit, utilizing their math workbooks, texts, and/or manipulatives, using the ***Learning Language Arts Through Literature*** series, completing typing exercises, practicing handwriting skills, brushing up on *spelling dragons*, studying Greek and Latin Roots (perhaps using Joel Lundquist's, ***English from the Roots Up***), playing educational games, reading classics, and so forth.

Then undertake a planned unit study spanning the next five-week period in which you integrate the skills you practiced into your own unit of study. Conducting these Basic Skills Units throughout the year will help to give you a base from which to formulate lessons to accompany your unit studies.

A good composition/grammar handbook will be a treasured resource for conducting your literary exercises. I recommend ***Write Source 2000*** and the ***Write Source 2000 Teacher's Guide***. These manuals cover nearly every aspect of writing including writing plays, poetry, journals, paragraphs, essays, phase biographies, phase

Conducting these Basic Skills Units throughout the year will help to give you a base from which to formulate lessons to accompany your unit studies.

autobiographies, news stories, stories, classroom reports, business letters, friendly letters, and more. They also contain significant information about the use of punctuation, spelling, capitalization, grammar, Greek and Latin roots, using the library, and so on. You'll find other interesting data such as the manual sign alphabet, cuneiform, Morse code, semaphore, the periodic chart of elements, a chart of the solar system, maps, calendars, etc.! (After I gave a similar description of **Write Source 2000** at a unit study seminar, one mother stood up in the back of the room and shouted, "Sold!")

Although the teacher's guide is not mandatory, it is useful for those formulating their own language arts exercises to coincide with a unit of study. These guides are recommended by the publisher for 6th through 8th grades, however, I say they are for people! I use them myself and am able to utilize the information gleaned to help even my four-year-old daughter. Highschoolers may prefer the next level up in the series, **Writer's Inc.**, which also has a teacher's guide available entitled, **Inc. Sights.** Another helpful resource for writing effectively is **The Clear and Simple Thesaurus Dictionary**, published by Grosset and Dunlap.

As I mentioned in a previous chapter, I like to acquaint myself with one or two books on a given topic and make good use of them. If I buy a composition/grammar handbook designed for each age/ grade level I am teaching, I will never become sufficiently familiar with any of them to use them effectively. This goes for the children as well. If they become acquainted with a reference book they can refer to year after year, they will reap a harvest of benefits. A familiar friend is one that is turned to again and again.

If they become acquainted with a reference book they can refer to year after year, they will reap a harvest of benefits.

CHAPTER NINE
There's More to Language than Meets the Ear

There's More to Language than Meets the Ear

Let's saunter back to the path we traversed in the last chapter as I discussed excerpts included in our ***Reader's Journals*** from ***The Story of My Life by Helen Keller***. Helen's limitations can also be used to help us realize that there's more to language than meets the ear. This concept is illustrated in the following passages by Helen Keller:

The deaf and the blind find it very difficult to acquire the amenities of conversation. How much more this difficulty must be augmented in the case of those who are both deaf and blind! They cannot distinguish the tone of the voice or, without assistance, go up and down the gamut of tones that give significance to words; nor can they watch the expression of the speaker's face, and a look is often the very soul of what one says.[17]

Following the inclusion of this passage in our ***Reader's Journal***, we can perform a simple exercise to help us visualize Helen's words. Read an excerpt from a well known children's story, such as ***Goldilocks and the Three Bears***, and employ no expression in either facial features or tone of voice. Make your voice very bland, almost robotic, and your face dull and placid. Then read the selection again, adding expression in both voice and countenance. Have the children compare the two readings.

As we are concentrating on the tone of voice and expression, I would like to share a thought provoking passage from ***A Family Program for Reading Aloud***, published by Foundation for American Christian Education. Noah Webster, in his Introduction to the Origin of Language in the ***1828 American Dictionary of the English Language*** states:

It is therefore probable that "language" as well as the faculty of speech, was the "immediate gift of God." This gift includes the "Voice," source of sound, "Tone," or accent and

It is therefore probable that "language" as well as the faculty of speech, was the "immediate gift of God."

inflection of the voice, and "Expression," that which identifies the ideas, convictions, and feelings of the speaker. These three elements are both internal and external. They make the difference between reading aloud that is monotonous and difficult to listen to, and that which is modulated. Modulation refers to "the act of inflecting the voice in reading or speaking; a rising or falling of the voice." This becomes the instrument of the Reader. If you love what you are reading; if you are interested in arousing the feelings of your listeners; if you know the message of the author and you wish to help convey it; all of these aspects will help you to use your voice effectively.[18]

CHAPTER TEN
*Authors that Encourage Us to Cultivate
a Special Relationship with Nature*

Authors that Encourage Us to Cultivate a Special Relationship with Nature

One of my favorite teachers is Charlotte Mason, who taught in England and lived from 1842 to 1923. She authored a number of books which have been reprinted in recent years including, **Home Education**. Her ageless methods offer us a vast wealth of knowledge bearing careful meditation. Among her many suggestions is the implementation and development of a special awareness and relationship with nature.

Through this relationship, we are directed to the one who orchestrates the wonders and complexities of nature. It is interesting to me that Helen Keller's teacher, Anne Sullivan, also realized the importance of this special relationship to be cultivated. The following excerpt from **The Story of My Life**, illustrates this point:

We read and studied out of doors, preferring the sunlit woods to the house. All my early lessons have in them the breath of the woods — the fine, resinous odour of pine needles, blended with the perfume of wild grapes. Seated in the gracious shade of a wild tulip tree, I learned to think that everything has a lesson and a suggestion. "The loveliness of things taught me all their use." Indeed, everything that could hum, or buzz, or sing, or bloom, had a part in my education — noisy-throated frogs, katydids and crickets held in my hand until, forgetting their embarrassment, they trilled their reedy note, little downy chickens and wildflowers, the dogwood blossoms, meadow-violets and budding fruit trees. I felt the bursting cotton-bolls and fingered their soft fiber and fuzzy seeds; I felt the low soughing of the wind through the cornstalks, the silky rustling of the long leaves, and the indignant snort of my pony, as we caught him in the pasture and put the bit in his mouth — ah me! how well I remember the spicy, clovery smell of his breath![19]

All my early lessons have in them the breath of the woods — the fine, resinous odour of pine needles, blended with the perfume of wild grapes.

Jessica Hulcey, co-author of the popular KONOS Character Curriculum, encourages the implementation of "discovery learning" techniques with children. It's exciting for me to see that Anne Sullivan was a proponent of the method of "discovery learning" as well.

Our favourite walk was to Keller's Landing, an old tumble-down lumber-wharf on the Tennessee River, used during the Civil War to land soldiers. There we spent many happy hours and played at learning geography. I built dams of pebbles, made islands and lakes, and dug river-beds, all for fun, and never dreamed that I was learning a lesson. I listened with increasing wonder to Miss Sullivan's descriptions of the great round world with its burning mountains, buried cities, moving rivers of ice, and many other things as strange. She made raised maps in clay, so that I could feel the mountain ridges and valleys, and follow with my fingers the devious course of rivers.[20]

Those using the *Greenleaf Guides to History*, will find that they offer instruction in creating salt maps of Egypt, Greece, Rome, and so forth.

There are a number of fine authors who have helped us to cultivate a relationship with nature. As we read the tales of Beatrix Potter and investigate her life through biographies, we find that she was an avid nature student. This special bond she possessed with nature aided her in making effective, true-to-life drawings of wood and creatures. Although her creatures took on human characteristics, it is obvious she studied real specimens to create her illustrations. Her stories began as illustrated letters to her dear friend's children when they were ill. Friends and family encouraged her to publish these in book form. (Keep this in mind when reading the next chapter.)

Jim Arnosky, a modern day naturalist, offers us inspiring glimpses into the natural world. Effective drawing instruction will assist even young artists. Arnosky's easy readers, focusing on raccoons, foxes, and other wildlife, encourage young readers to take a closer look at the wonders of creation while offering them simple, but interesting beginning reading material. You may be able to find these books in your public library. (For a listing of books by Jim Arnosky, see the Recommended Book List on page 84.)

It is fascinating to me how authors (and illustrators) use their gifts to introduce little known or unexplored areas of life and give us in-depth knowledge to further pursue those areas of interest.

Quoting once again from *A Family Program for Reading Aloud*, published by the Foundation for American Christian Education:

But there are other purposes in the teaching and learning of literature. One of these purposes is to minister to the individual student. Through skillful teachers who are able to inspire and delight the mind and heart, new horizons are opened up, and new fields envisioned which provide challenge. The wider the range of reading, and the more focused, the greater are the opportunities for self-discovery.

The purpose of reading in a specific field is to extend the horizons of our mind to contemplate the implications of a particular subject.[21]

Through skillful teachers who are able to inspire and delight the mind and heart, new horizons are opened up, and new fields envisioned which provide challenge.

CHAPTER ELEVEN
Learning from Letters

Learning from Letters

I find it fascinating to read the letters included at the end of Helen Keller's autobiography. Some of these letters were written by Helen at different stages in her childhood, others were written to Helen by various individuals. As we are on the subject of letters, I would like to share a little of the importance of letters. In our day of mass communication, letter writing is becoming a dying art. It seems to me that in general, people write less and less as they are occupied more and more with mechanical distractions.

If we observe biographies that we read in the course of our studies, we find that letters, diaries, journals, and other writings such as these provide the foundation of much of the person's life story. (Read the bibliography located at the end of each biography for a listing of the supportive materials.) It is important to point out to our children the significance of the written word. The Bible is our Heavenly Father's letter of love to us. "Thy word is a lamp unto my feet and a light unto my path."

Returning our thoughts to the letters following Helen's autobiography, let's look at what we can learn from them. As illustrated in this next quote from *The Story of My Life*, we understand how difficult it is for a deaf child to acquire language.

This process was continued for several years; for the deaf child does not learn in a month, or even in two or three years, the numberless idioms and expressions used in the simplest daily intercourse. The little hearing child learns these from constant repetition and imitation. The conversation he hears in his home stimulates his mind and suggests topics and calls forth the spontaneous expression of his own thoughts. This natural exchange of ideas is denied to the deaf child.[22]

It is amazing to me that at the writing of her autobiography at age 22, Helen possessed the ability to skillfully express her thoughts and ideas although encumbered by almost overwhelming physical hindrances. It is helpful to look at her earlier years, when the mystery

If we observe biographies that we read in the course of our studies, we find that letters, diaries, journals, and other writings such as these provide the foundation of much of the person's life story. It is important to point out to our children the significance of the written word.

of language was newly disclosed to her.

Miss Sullivan began to teach Helen Keller on March 3rd, 1887. Three months and a half after her first word was spelled into her hand, she wrote in pencil this letter.
TO HER COUSIN ANNA (MRS. GEORGE T. TURNER)
(Tuscumbia, Alabama, June 17, 1887.)
helen write anna george will give helen apple simpson will shoot bird jack will give helen stick of candy doctor will give mildred medicine mother will make mildred new dress
(No signature)[23]

It is remarkable to see the progression from one letter to the next.

By the following September Helen shows improvement in fullness of construction and more extended relations of thought.[24]

The following is a short excerpt from a letter Helen wrote to her teacher while Miss Sullivan was away. This letter was written only two years after her first. Note the improvement in all areas of style, vocabulary, composition, and sentence structure.
TO MISS ANNE MANSFIELD SULLIVAN
Tuscumbia, Alabama, August 7, 1889.
Dearest Teacher — I am very glad to write to you this evening, for I have been thinking much about you all day. I am sitting on the piazza, and my little white pigeon is perched on the back of my chair, watching me write. Her little brown mate has flown away with the other birds; but Annie is not sad, for she likes to stay with me.[25]

As we read these letters with our children, we can make comparisons between them. It's this sort of comparing and contrasting of writings that develops and nurtures our thinking skills. Children are beckoned to offer their thoughts and inspirations about a matter, rather than to read a paragraph and then select the best answer from a multiple choice listing. Much of this discussion can take place orally and gradually develop into written essays.

It's this sort of comparing and contrasting of writings that develops and nurtures our thinking skills.

Turning our discussion back to Helen's letters:

Helen Keller's letters are important, not only as a supplementary story of her life, but as a demonstration of her growth in thought and expression — the growth which in itself has made her distinguished.

One cause for the excellence of her letters is the great number of them. They are the exercises which have trained her to write.[26]

Another excerpt taken from the collection of Helen's letters reads:

Like a good many of Helen Keller's early letters, this to her French teacher is her re-phrasing of a story. It shows how much the gift of writing is, in the early stages of its development, the gift of mimicry.[27]

And so these two quotes emphasize two very important methods utilized in good writing instruction. It's evident that exercises comprised of copying, dictation, and narration (a retelling or rephrasing of what's been read), offer excellent training in writing. It is also important to spend sufficient time writing, as Helen did. Writing letters were the exercises that trained her to write.

We can glean a bit of history as we read Helen's autobiography and the letters she both wrote and received. She was intimately acquainted with Dr. Alexander Graham Bell at an early age. Dr. Bell was greatly responsible for encouraging Helen's education. She recollects her first encounter with this great man.

Child as I was, I at once felt the tenderness and sympathy which endeared Dr. Bell to so many hearts, as his wonderful achievements enlist their admiration. He held me on his knee while I examined his watch, and he made it strike for me. He understood my signs, and I knew it and loved him at once. But I did not dream that that interview would be the door through which I should pass from darkness into light, from isolation to friendship, companionship, knowledge, love.

Dr. Bell advised my father to write to Mr. Anagnos,

It is also important to spend sufficient time writing, as Helen did.

director of the Perkins Institution in Boston, the scene of Dr. Howe's great labours for the blind, and ask him if he had a teacher competent to begin my education.[28]

We chose a short biography of Dr. Alexander Graham Bell to read after we encountered him in Helen's life story. We selected a newer biography filled with excellent photographs, including a photograph of Helen and Anne Sullivan with Dr. Bell. The children and I were excited to see them pictured together. We didn't launch an in-depth study of Dr. Bell and his accomplishments at this time as I wanted our focus to remain on our initial study of sign language, however, investigating Dr. Bell briefly at this point added a significant dimension to our study.

Later, when we conduct a unit study more intensely focused on Dr. Bell, his accomplishments, and his inventions, we will be able to say, "Oh yes, we remember that Alexander Graham Bell and Helen Keller were friends. Dr. Bell played an important part in Helen's education."

Several letters between Dr. Bell and Helen are included in the afterward of Helen's life story. Helen even dedicated her autobiography to Dr. Bell:

TO ALEXANDER GRAHAM BELL
Who has taught the deaf to speak and enabled the listening ear to hear speech from the Atlantic to the Rockies,
I DEDICATE
This Story of My Life.[29]

There were several other famous individuals that we encountered along with Helen. She wrote and received letters from prominent persons such as John Greenleaf Whitier, Dr. Oliver Wendell Holmes, Rev. Phillip Brooks, Mrs. Grover Cleveland, Dr. Edward Everette Hale, and others.

It is this personal encounter of individual with individual that helps us to see history as it truly is, not a series of dates and wars to be memorized, but a series of relationships between people, places, ideas, and events. History comes alive as we feel the sufferings, joys,

History comes alive as we feel the sufferings, joys, defeats, and accomplishments of people throughout time.

defeats, and accomplishments of people throughout time.

Although not every autobiography or biography we read will offer as much food for thought as *The Story of My Life*, by Helen Keller, it is easy to see that unit studies, based on the lives, triumphs, and sorrows of real people, in real space and time gives us a more enthralling picture than dry textbooks. We should provide a vast supply of good books for our children to read and listen to. For as Gladys Hunt states in the book she co-authored, *Read for Your Life*:

Good stories put flesh on abstract ideas. It's difficult to fathom what it means to be noble, valiant, courageous, or even unselfish, unless we meet people in stories whose actions show us what these things mean.

We learn how to use the English language when we read good writing. It's a by-product. We come to admire the right word in the right place — and we are amazed at what it can convey.[30]

A good writer has something worth saying and says it in the best possible way and respects the reader's ability to understand. Language is used well. The word choices make us see, feel, hear, taste, smell, decide. The action of the story and the descriptions have a crisp leanness because strong verbs and simple descriptions are used. The Bible is a model for this kind of writing. With an economy of words, lasting pictures are painted.[31]

There's so much more I would like to share that we learned while reading the autobiography of Miss Keller, but space does not allow and it is better that you and your children have the opportunity to newly discover these gems for yourselves. (For a listing of other books and materials utilized and activities conducted during our Sign Language Unit, please see my book, *The Unit Study Idea Book*.)

I hope these excerpts will help you to see how we conduct our studies and how our *Reader's Journals* contribute to our love for reading and our life-long habit of reading. For it isn't profitable to just bury our noses in books, we must be able to learn from these

It's difficult to fathom what it means to be noble, valiant, courageous, or even unselfish, unless we meet people in stories whose actions show us what these things mean.

For it isn't profitable to just bury our noses in books, we must be able to learn from these books and act upon the knowledge gained.

books and act upon the knowledge gained. Furthermore, reading leads to writing which enables us to enjoy communication and self-expression in a vital way.

RECOMMENDED BOOK LIST

The Clear and Simple Thesaurus Dictionary,
by Harriet Wittels and Joan Greisman,
Published by Grosset & Dunlap (1971), New York, NY.

Games for Reading: Playful Ways to Help Your Child Read,
by Peggy Kaye, Published by Pantheon Books (1984),
a division of Random House Publishers, New York, NY.

Read for Your Life: Turning Teens into Readers,
by Gladys Hunt and Barbara Hampton,
Published by Zondervan (1992), Grand Rapids, MI.

Books Children Love: A Guide to the Best Children's Literature,
by Elizabeth Wilson, Published by Crossway Books (1987), Westchester, IL.

Honey for a Child's Heart: The Imaginative Use of Books in Family Life, by Gladys Hunt,
Published by Zondervan (1989), Grand Rapids, MI.

Let the Authors Speak: A Guide to Worthy Books Based on Historical Setting, by Carolyn Hatcher,
Published by Old Pinnacle Publishing (1992), Joelton, TN.

Home Education: Training and Educating Children Under Nine,
by Charlotte Mason Vol.1 of the Original Home Schooling Series
(6 Vols.) Published by Tyndale House (1989), Wheaton, IL.

Learning Language Arts Through Literature series: Including, *The Common Sense Reading Program*,
Published by Common Sense Press, Melrose, FL.

Green Leaf Guides to History, by Rob and Cyndy Shearer;
English for the Thoughtful Child, by Cyndy Shearer;
Published by Green Leaf Press, Lebanon, TN.

Write Source 2000, *Write Source 2000 Teacher's Guide*,
Writer's Inc., and *Inc. Sights: Teacher's Guide for Writer's Inc.*,
Published by Write Source Publishing House, Burlington, WI.

The Story of My Life, by Helen Keller,
Published by Bantam Books (1990), New York, NY.

A Picture Book of Helen Keller, by David A. Adler,
Published by Holiday House, New York, NY.

A Deaf Child Listened, by Anne E. Neimark,
Published by William Morrow and Company, New York, NY.

A Family Program for Reading Aloud, by Rosalie June Slater (1991),
2nd Edition; *Mother Carey's Chickens*, by Kate Douglas Wiggin (1910),
republished in 1991; *Joel: A Boy of Galilee*, by Annie Fellows Johnston
(1898), republished in 1992; Published by the Foundation for American
Christian Education San Francisco, CA.

The Natural Speller, by Kathyrn Stout,
Published by Design-A-Study, Wilmington, DE.

Simply Grammar, by Karen Andreola, Published by
The Charlotte Mason Research and Supply Company, Eugene, OR.

Little Women, by Louisa May Alcott, Distributed by Outlet Books,
a division of Random House Publishers, Westminster, MD.

Dangerous Journey, by John Bunyan, edited by Oliver Hunkin,
Published by Wm. B. Eerdmans Publishing Company, Grand Rapids, MI.

Secrets of a Wildlife Watcher, *Drawing from Nature*, *Crinkleroot's
Guide to Knowing the Trees*, *Crinkleroot's Guide to Walking in
Wild Places*, *Crinkleroot's Book of Animal Tracking*, *Crinkleroot's
guide to Knowing the Birds*, *Raccoons and Ripe Corn* (Early
Reader), *Deer at the Brook* (Early Reader), *Come Out, Muskrats*
(Early Reader), *Watching Foxes* (Early Reader),
all by Jim Arnosky, Published by Beech Tree Books, a division of William
Morrow & Company, New York, NY.

The Evergreen Wood,
by Alan and Linda Parry, Published by Oliver-Nelson Books,
a division of Thomas Nelson, Inc., Publishers, Nashville, TN.

How to Create Your Own Unit Study, *The Unit Study Idea Book*,
Success with Unit Studies, *Creating Books with Children*, *How to
Create Your Own Unit Study 90-Minute Audio Cassette Tape*, *For
the Love of Reading,* and *The Frances Study Guide* by Valerie Bendt,
Published by Common Sense Press, Melrose, FL.

ACKNOWLEDGEMENTS

Portions taken from *The Story of My Life*, by Helen Keller, are taken from the Bantam 1990 edition. Bantam Doubleday Dell Publishing Group, Inc., 666 Fifth Avenue, New York, NY 10103.

Portions taken from *Honey for a Child's Heart*, by Gladys Hunt, are used with permission by Zondervan Publishing House, Grand Rapids, MI 49530.

Portions taken from *Read for Your Life: Turning Teens into Readers*, by Gladys Hunt and Barbara Hampton, are used with permission by Zondervan Publishing House, Grand Rapids, MI 49530.

Portions taken from *The Elements of Grammar*, by Margaret Shertzer, are used with permission by Macmillan Publishing Company, 886 Third Avenue, New York, NY 10022.

Portions taken from *A Family Program for Reading Aloud*, by Rosalie June Slater, 2nd Edition, are used with permission by Foundation for American Christian Education, P.O. Box 27035, San Francisco, CA 94127.

Portions taken from *Let the Authors Speak*, by Carolyn Hatcher, are used with permission by Old Pinnacle Publishing, P. O. Box 698, Joelton, TN 37080.

Portions taken from *Gallaudet: Friend of the Deaf*, by Etta DeGering, are taken from the edition published by David McKay Company, Inc., New York, NY.

Portions from *Little Women*, by Louisa may Alcott, are taken from the edition published by Outlet Books, a division of Random House Publishers, Avenel, NJ.

REFERENCES

1. *Games for Math*, Peggy Kaye, author of *Games for Reading*, introduction.

2. *Little Women,* by Louisa May Alcott, 1987 edition, distributed by Outlet Book Company, Inc., a Random House Company, p. 3.

3. *Little Women*, by Louisa May Alcott, 1987 edition, distributed by Outlet Books Company, Inc., a Random House Company, p. 9.

4. *Little Women*, by Louisa May Alcott, 1987 edition, distributed by Outlet Book Company, Inc., a Random House Company, p. 9.

5. *Little Women*, by Louisa May Alcott, 1987 edition, distributed by Outlet Book Company, Inc., a Random House Company, p. 10.

6. *Little Women*, by Louisa May Alcott, 1987 edition, distributed by Outlet Book Company, Inc., a Random House Company, p. 10.

7. *Little Women*, by Louisa May Alcott, 1987 edition, distributed by Outlet Book Company, Inc., a Random House Company, p. 12.

8. *Honey For a Child's Heart*, by Gladys Hunt, p. 13-14.

9. *Let the Authors Speak*, by Carolyn Hatcher, p. 23.

10. *The Story of My Life*, by Helen Keller, Bantam 1990 edition, p. 14.

11. *The Story of My Life*, by Helen Keller, Bantam 1990 edition, p. 16.

12. *The Story of My Life*, by Helen Keller, Bantam 1990 edition, p. 17.

13. *The Story of My Life*, by Helen Keller, Bantam 1990 edition, p. 84-85.

14. *Gallaudet, Friend of the Deaf*, by Etta DeGering, p. 40-43.

15. *The Story of My Life*, by Helen Keller, Bantam 1990 edition, p. 18.

16. *The Elements of Grammar*, by Margaret Shertzer, p. 2.

17. *The Story of My Life*, by Helen Keller, Bantam 1990 edition, p. 23.

18. *A Family Program for Reading Aloud*, by Rosalie J. Slater, p. 5.

19. *The Story of My Life*, by Helen Keller, Bantam 1990 edition, p. 24-25.

20. *The Story of My Life*, by Helen Keller, Bantam 1990 edition, p. 25.

21. *A Family Program for Reading Aloud*, by Rosalie J. Slater, p. 61-62.

22. *The Story of My Life*, by Helen Keller, Bantam 1990 edition, p. 22.

23. *The Story of My Life*, by Helen Keller, Bantam 1990 edition, p. 115.

24. *The Story of My Life*, by Helen Keller, Bantam 1990 edition, p. 116.

25. *The Story of My Life*, by Helen Keller, Bantam 1990 edition, p. 137.

26. *The Story of My Life*, by Helen Keller, Bantam 1990 edition, p. 109.

[27] ***The Story of My Life***, by Helen Keller, Bantam 1990 edition, p. 135.

[28] ***The Story of My Life***, by Helen Keller, Bantam 1990 edition, p. 13.

[29] ***The Story of My Life***, by Helen Keller, Bantam 1990 edition, dedication page.

[30] ***Read for Your Life***, by Gladys Hunt and Barbara Hampton, p. 17-18.

[31] ***Read for Your Life***, by Gladys Hunt and Barbara Hampton, p. 43.

NOTES